D0622944

21st Century Skills Library

REAL WORLD MATH: SPORTS
FOOTBALL

Katie Marsico and Cecilia Minden

Cherry Lake Publishing
Ann Arbor, Michigan

Published in the United States of America by Cherry Lake Publishing
Ann Arbor, Michigan
www.cherrylakepublishing.com

Math Adviser: Tonya Walker, MA, Boston University

Content Adviser: Thomas Sawyer, EdD, Professor of Recreation and Sport
Management, Indiana State University

Photo Credits: Cover and page 1, ©GPI Stock/Alamy; page 4, ©iStockphoto.com/groveb; page 7,
©Ace Stock Limited/Alamy; page 8, ©hanzl, used under license from Shutterstock, Inc.; page 10,
©iStockphoto.com/surpasspro; page 12, ©Daniel Padavona, used under license from Shutterstock,
Inc.; page 15, ©Robbins Photography; pages 17 and 22, ©Joe Robbins; page 18, ©AP Photo/Mark
Gilliland; page 20, ©AP Photo; page 24, ©iStockphoto.com/BirdofPrey; page 27, ©Jeff Greenberg/
Alamy; page 28, ©MWProductions, used under license from Shutterstock, Inc.

Library of Congress Cataloging-in-Publication Data
Marsico, Katie, 1980–
 Football / by Katie Marsico and Cecilia Minden.
   p. cm.—(Real world math)
 Includes bibliographical references and index.
 ISBN-13: 978-1-60279-247-0
 ISBN-10: 1-60279-247-X
 1. Football—Juvenile literature. 2. Arithmetic—Problems, exercises,
etc.—Juvenile literature. I. Minden, Cecilia. II. Title. III. Series.
 GV950.7.M27 2009
 796.33—dc22   2008001165

*Cherry Lake Publishing would like to acknowledge the work of
The Partnership for 21st Century Skills.
Please visit* www.21stcenturyskills.org *for more information.*

TABLE OF CONTENTS

CHAPTER ONE
Touchdown!   4

CHAPTER TWO
A Few Football Basics   8

CHAPTER THREE
Do the Math: Impressive Pros   15

CHAPTER FOUR
Do the Math: Remarkable NFL Records   20

CHAPTER FIVE
Get Your Game Going!   24

Real World Math Challenge Answers   29

Glossary   30

For More Information   31

Index   32

About the Authors   32

TOUCHDOWN!

Football is a contact sport that requires good running and ball handling skills.

Your heart is pumping as you run across the football field. You hold the ball tightly to your chest. The crowd cheers as you speed toward the other team's end zone. Your **opponents** are determined to keep you from scoring. No one can stop you as you race across the goal line.

Touchdown! Your team has won the game! Your teammates gather around you for high fives. You are a talented athlete, but that was not all that helped you today. Would you believe that you also needed math skills to be a winner on the football field?

REAL WORLD MATH CHALLENGE

Juan scores 3 touchdowns during a school football game. His team scores a total of 25 points. **How many points does Juan score for his team? How many points do other players score? What percentage of the total points does Juan score?** Hint: Each touchdown is worth 6 points.

(Turn to page 29 for the answers)

How important is math to football? First, you need to know the history of the game. Football has been around in some form since **ancient** times. Experts believe that people in Greece and China were playing football more than 2,000 years ago. The sport became popular in Western Europe in the 1300s. Different countries also developed their own versions of the game. These included sports such as rugby and soccer.

Learning & Innovation Skills

Football grew more popular as a sport in England in the late 1700s and early 1800s. Entire villages often played one another on holidays. Such games had few rules. Lines didn't mark end zones as they do today. Sometimes players moved the ball through town streets and across streams! People began working together to establish official rules. This helped them avoid having to learn new guidelines every time they played. The rules for football may have changed over the years, but players still play hard!

American football today got its start in the late 1800s. It quickly became a popular game.

Professional football in the United States began in 1892. The American Professional Football Association (APFA) was created in 1920. The APFA changed its name to the National Football League (NFL) in 1922. A similar league called the American Football League (AFL) was formed in 1960. The AFL became part of the NFL in 1970.

The NFL is currently the country's largest professional football league. It includes 32 teams. The NFL is made up of two separate groups called the National Football Conference (NFC) and the

American Football Conference (AFC). Teams play one another from August through January. The two best teams from the NFC and AFC then compete in a popular winter game known as the Super

Equipment and uniforms have changed over the years, but it still takes talent, hard work, and dedication to make it to the NFL.

Bowl. The winner of the Super Bowl is declared that year's NFL champion.

Now you know a little about the history of American football. You are ready to learn the rules of the game. You are also ready to find out how math comes into play on the field. Just grab your helmet and your calculator!

CHAPTER TWO

A FEW FOOTBALL BASICS

You need math skills to understand the game of football.

Football is not just about kicking, throwing, and running. Football also uses measurements and math. The game is played on a field that is 120 yards (110 meters) long and 53 yards (49 m) wide. There are several white lines painted on the field. Each line has a different meaning.

Boundary lines that run the length of the field are called sidelines. Those that run the width of the field are called end lines. Hash marks are lines painted near the middle of the field. Every play begins on or between the hash marks. Yard lines stretch between the sidelines every 5 yards (4.6 m). The 50-yard line marks the middle of the field. The lines on a football field help players understand how close they are to scoring a goal.

A goal line is also painted at either end of the field. The goal is called an end zone. The end zone covers an area that is 10 yards (9.1 m) from the goal line to the end line. Two goalposts stand near the back of each end zone. These posts are 18.5 feet (5.6 m) apart from one another. Why is it so important that football players pay attention to all these measurements?

Only 11 players from each team are allowed on the field at once. Each team has control of the ball at different points in the game. The team

Teams calculate how many yards they need to make on each play.

with the ball is playing **offense**. They are trying to score. The team without the ball is playing **defense**.

They are trying to get the ball back and stop the offense from scoring.

Every play in football begins at an imaginary line called the line of scrimmage. This line is placed wherever the ball ended up after the last play. Players from opposing teams face each other at the line of scrimmage before a new play begins. The offense starts the play by snapping the ball or hiking it.

The offensive team starts out with four downs. This means they have four chances to move the ball at least 10 yards (9.1 m) toward the end zone. The offensive team must advance the ball this distance or farther. Then they are given a fresh set of downs. If the offense cannot move the ball at least 10 yards after four downs, the ball goes to the defense.

The offense can score in a number of ways. The offense can kick a field goal through the goalposts. Field goals are worth three points. The offense can also score a touchdown. Touchdowns are made by either passing or running the ball into the end zone. A touchdown is worth six points.

In 2007, the AFC's New England Patriots achieved perfection. They won every game during the regular season, ending with a record of 16-0. Only one other team in history was able to accomplish that feat. Football is a tough and physical sport. Success takes the strength of an entire team. Collaboration and teamwork helped the New England Patriots achieve victory.

not tackling someone who doesn't have the ball. Players aren't allowed to

hurt anyone on purpose. It is also against the rules to grab or touch each

other's face masks.

REAL WORLD MATH CHALLENGE

Mia and Sam want to play a game of football. Their game has four 15-minute quarters. It also includes a 10-minute halftime and 8 minutes in time-outs. **How long does their game last? What percentage of time do they spend actually playing?**

(Turn to page 29 for the answers)

A player commits a foul in football when he breaks a rule. A player who

is responsible for a foul might be removed from the game. Referees often

punish teams that commit fouls. These punishments sometimes involve

giving an advantage to the other team. Players who understand the rules

use them to succeed!

CHAPTER THREE

DO THE MATH: IMPRESSIVE PROS

NFL stars awe fans with their amazing performances on the field. Walter Payton is a perfect example. Payton was a running back for the Chicago Bears from 1975 to 1987. His job was to run with the ball and score. He set several NFL records during his career. He rushed for

Walter Payton played his entire pro football career for the Chicago Bears.

16,726 yards (15,294 m) and scored 110 touchdowns. Payton retired as the leading rusher in NFL history in 1987. He was inducted into the Pro Football Hall of Fame in 1993. He had missed only one game in 13 years!

There will never be another NFL star quite like Payton, but other offensive players continue to make names for themselves. In 2007, New England Patriots quarterback Tom Brady broke NFL records with 50 touchdown passes during a single season. Emmitt Smith is a former running back for the Dallas Cowboys and the Arizona Cardinals. He broke many of Payton's records and was named the NFL's leading rusher in 2002.

The NFL has many record-setting defensive players, too. Bruce Smith was a defensive end for the Buffalo Bills and the Washington Redskins. His job was to line up at the end of the defensive line and stop any offensive

REAL WORLD MATH CHALLENGE

Walter Payton rushed for 16,726 yards (15,294 m) and scored 110 touchdowns. Emmitt Smith rushed for 18,355 yards (16,784 m) and scored 164 touchdowns. **How many more yards did Smith rush than Payton? How many more touchdowns did Smith score?**

(Turn to page 29 for the answers)

plays. He was known for the way he exploded off the line of scrimmage and into the action. Upon retiring in 2003, he held an NFL record of 200 career sacks. A sack is when a defensive player tackles a quarterback behind the line of scrimmage.

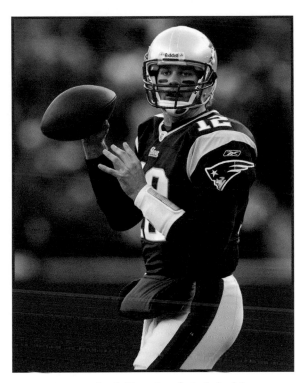

Quarterback Tom Brady led the New England Patriots to three Super Bowl victories before his 28th birthday.

Safety Bob Sanders of the AFC's Indianapolis Colts is another defensive player who has been amazing NFL fans. A safety is a type of defensive back. Sanders was named NFL Defensive Player of the Year in 2007. His skills stopped opposing teams from scoring more than 262 points against the Colts that season.

The National Women's Football Association was formed in August 2000.

NFL players are honored for their athletic talent in different ways. Some are named Most Valuable Player (MVP) or Player of the Year. Numbers that show how many times athletes score or how often they stop other teams from scoring add to their fame.

These numbers also affect the numbers on players' paychecks. Most NFL stars earn large salaries. Leonard Davis is a good example of an NFL player who makes a lot of money. He is an offensive player for the Cowboys and earned $26,325,720 from June 2006 to June 2007. Who wouldn't like to mix math and sports to get a number like that?

21st Century Content

The NFL is made up of only male athletes, but that does not mean women don't play football. The Independent Women's Football League (IWFL) includes more than 1,000 players on 30 teams across North America. Similar groups exist all over the continent. They include the National Women's Football Association (NWFA), the Women's Football League (WFL), and the Women's Professional Football League (WPFL). Such leagues give women a chance to play organized, official games and prove their athletic talent to the world. There is also an alternate men's league called the Arena Football League. This league is quickly becoming popular.

Why do you think the IWFL, NWFA, WFL, WPFL, and Arena Football League are not as well known as the NFL? What do you think the league owners could do to make their teams more popular?

REAL WORLD MATH CHALLENGE

If Leonard Davis earns $26 million each year, **how much money will he have made between June 2007 and June 2010?**

(Turn to page 29 for the answer)

CHAPTER FOUR

Do the Math: Remarkable NFL Records

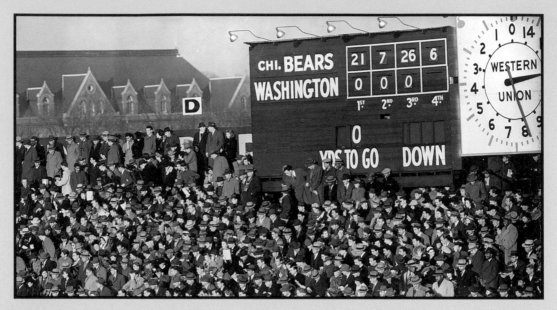

The scoreboard shows the Bears leading the Redskins in the fourth quarter of their December 8, 1940 game. The Bears won with a record-setting score of 73-0.

Many football fans will always remember a game between the Chicago Bears and the Washington Redskins on December 8, 1940. Why was it so special? It still holds the record 68 years later for the most points scored in a single game. The Bears defeated the Redskins 73–0. This is also a record for the most points earned in a shutout. A shutout is a game in which one team fails to score.

Football is filled with records. Some are related to specific players. Others deal with teams, games, or seasons. The AFC's New England Patriots hold the record for the most points scored by a team in a single season. Players earned 561 points in 2007. The Patriots also set a record for being the most recent team to win every game in one season. They claimed 16 victories in 2007.

REAL WORLD MATH CHALLENGE

The NFC's Arizona Cardinals hold the record for the most field goals scored in a single season. They had 43 in 2005. The Patriots hold the record for scoring the most touchdowns in a season. They made 71 in 2007. **How many points did the Cardinals gain in earning their record? How many points did the Patriots score in achieving their record? Which team scored more points by setting these records?** (Remember that a field goal is worth 3 points and a touchdown is worth 6 points.)

(Turn to page 29 for the answers)

The Carolina Panthers line up during a game in 2007.

Not every NFL record is related to winning. Some records deal with

defeat. The NFC's Carolina Panthers hold the most recent record for

the greatest number of losses in a single season. They were defeated 15

times in 2001. The AFC's Kansas City Chiefs hold the record for the most

penalties earned in one season. They received 158 in 1998.

There are even records that have nothing to do with winning or losing. The Bears hold a record for the most ties in a single season. They tied with six other teams in 1932. Three of those ties occurred one after another. So the Bears also have a record for the most **consecutive** ties!

The exciting thing about football is that every new game holds the possibility of new records. Numbers have the power to make people remember an athlete or sporting event for years to come. They are what shape football history!

The Indianapolis Colts proved that luck could change over the course of a year. The Colts hold the record for the largest single-season improvement in wins. They lost 13 games and won 3 in 1998. The Colts reversed those numbers in 1999 by losing 3 games and winning 13. Despite their rocky season in 1998, the Colts were able to move forward. How can a team make such a big improvement? Putting the past behind them, looking toward the future, and working hard to improve their game are skills any team needs to succeed on or off the playing field.

CHAPTER FIVE

GET YOUR GAME GOING!

Many young children play flag football and then move up to tackle football when they are older.

Y ou have learned how athletes in the NFL play football. Does that mean you have to be a professional star to enjoy the sport? No way! Many colleges, high schools, and grade schools have organized football teams. You can also simply play a game with friends or family members.

You might choose flag football or touch football if you are just playing for fun. Neither version of the game allows tackling. Flag football usually has two teams of eight players. Participants wear a belt with a flag around their waists. Members of the other team remove these flags instead of tackling. Touch football often features six players on each team. Participants lightly touch offensive players with one or both hands in place of tackling.

You will need a ball and a place to play after you finish dressing. You can choose from several different types of footballs. Most are made out of leather, rubber, plastic, or foam. You can purchase footballs at sports stores and toy stores.

Where is the best place to toss around the ball? Try to pick a wide-open space. Many people like to play in a grassy area such as a park or yard. An indoor athletic court also works for touch football or flag football. Be sure that whatever spot you choose is well lit. It should also be far enough away from busy streets and people who might accidentally wander onto the field and get hurt. Select an outdoor area that has more grass than concrete. You will probably have less chance of being injured if you fall or are tackled on grass.

Your field may not always feature the painted lines the NFL uses. You can instead rely on markers such as trees, playground equipment, or plastic

REAL WORLD MATH CHALLENGE

Kayla is saving up her money to buy a football. One of the balls she likes is $16.00. The other is $20.00. Kayla has an allowance of $4.00 a week. **What is the price difference between the two balls? How long will it take her to save enough money for the less expensive ball? How about for the more expensive one?**

(Turn to page 29 for the answers)

With a little creativity, almost any space can become a football field.

cones. For example, a sandbox might represent where the end zone begins.

A row of bushes might mark where a sideline runs.

There are many different ways to enjoy football. Maybe you like to

watch NFL games on Sunday afternoons. Perhaps you prefer to play touch

football with your family after dinner. Always keep in mind that this sport

*It takes a lot of practice and good math skills
to become an expert football player.*

is supposed to be fun. Also, remember that you are sure to have a winning

advantage if you use your math skills.

What are you waiting for? You have already practiced addition,

subtraction, multiplication, and division. Now it's time to score

some touchdowns!

REAL WORLD MATH CHALLENGE ANSWERS

Chapter One
Page 5

Juan scores a total of 18 points for his team.

3 touchdowns x 6 points = 18 points

The other players score 7 points.

25 points − 18 points = 7 points

Juan scores 72 percent of the points.

$18 \div 25 = 0.72 = 72\%$

Chapter Two
Page 14

Mia and Sam's game lasts 60 minutes.

4 quarters x 15 minutes = 60 minutes

With halftime and time-outs, the game lasts a total of 78 minutes.

60 minutes + 10 minutes + 8 minutes = 78 minutes

They spend 77 percent of that time actually playing.

$60 \div 78 = 0.77 = 77\%$

Chapter Three
Page 16

Smith rushed 1,629 more yards (1,490 m) than Payton.

18,355 yards − 16,726 yards = 1,629 yards

He made 54 more touchdowns rushing.

164 touchdowns − 110 touchdowns = 54 touchdowns

Page 19

There are 3 years between 2007 and 2010.

2010 − 2007 = 3 years

Davis will earn $78 million between 2007 and 2010.

3 years x $26 million = $78 million

Chapter Four
Page 21

The Cardinals gained 129 points earning their 2005 record.

43 field goals x 3 points = 129 points

The Patriots scored 426 points achieving their 2007 record.

71 touchdowns x 6 points = 426 points

The Patriots scored 297 more points with their 2007 record.

426 − 129 = 297 points

Chapter Five
Page 26

The price difference between the balls Kayla likes is $4.00.

$20.00 − $16.00 = $4.00

If she earns $4.00 a week, it will take her 4 weeks to save enough for the less expensive one.

$16.00 ÷ $4.00 = 4 weeks

It will take her 5 weeks to save enough for the more expensive ball.

$20.00 ÷ $4.00 = 5 weeks

GLOSSARY

advancing (ad-VANSS-ing) moving forward or toward a goal

ancient (AYN-shunt) dating back thousands of years

consecutive (kuhn-SEK-yuh-tiv) back-to-back or one after another

defense (DEE-fenss) a team that is attempting to prevent its opponents from scoring

intercept (in-tur-SEPT) to catch a ball being thrown by another team

offense (AW-fenss) a team that is attempting to score

opponents (uh-POH-nuhnts) players on the other side or opposite team

professional (pruh-FESH-uh-nuhl) describing a sport that is played for money or as a career

turf (TURF) a surface area that is often used by sports players and that is made up of grass and grass roots

FOR MORE INFORMATION

Books

Gigliotti, Jim. *Football Superstars*. Chanhassen, MN: Child's World, 2006.

Madden, John. *John Madden's Heroes of Football*. New York: Dutton, 2006.

Pellowski, Michael J. *The Little Giant Book of Football Facts*. New York: Sterling Publishing, 2007.

Web Sites

NFL Rush
www.nflrush.com
Visit the National Football League's interactive kids' site

Official Site of the National Football League
www.nfl.com
Get news, scores, and the latest updates from the NFL

Official Web Site of the Independent Women's Football League
www.iwflsports.com
Check out the IWFL and get the scoop on women's football

INDEX

50-yard line, 9

American Football Conference (AFC), 7, 11, 17, 22
American Football League (AFL), 6
American Professional Football Association (APFA), 6
Arena Football League, 19
Arizona Cardinals, 16, 21

Brady, Tom, 16

Carolina Panthers, 22
Chicago Bears, 15, 20, 23
China, 5
cleats, 13, 25

Davis, Leonard, 18–19
defense, 10, 11, 12, 16
downs, 11

end lines, 9
end zones, 4, 6, 9, 11, 12, 27
England, 6
equipment, 13, 25

face masks, 13, 14, 25
field goals, 11, 21
fields, 8–9, 25–27
flag football, 24–25
footballs, 25
fouls. See penalties.

goal lines, 4, 9
goalposts, 9, 11
Greece, 5

halftime, 13
hash marks, 9

Independent Women's Football League (IWFL), 19
Indianapolis Colts, 17, 23
interceptions, 12

Kansas City Chiefs, 22

line of scrimmage, 10, 13, 17

Minnesota Vikings, 21
Most Valuable Player (MVP) awards, 18

National Football Conference (NFC), 6, 7, 21, 22
National Football League (NFL), 6–7, 13, 15, 16, 17, 18, 19, 22
National Women's Football Association (NWFA), 19
New England Patriots, 11, 16, 21

offense, 10, 11, 12

Payton, Walter, 15, 16
penalties, 14, 22
Player of the Year awards, 17, 18
plays, 9, 10
points, 5, 11, 12, 17, 20–21
Pro Football Hall of Fame, 15

quarters, 13

records, 15, 16, 17, 20–23
referees, 13, 14

rugby, 5
rules, 6, 7, 13–14

sacks, 17
safeties, 17
safety equipment, 13, 25
salaries, 18–19
Sanders, Bob, 17
season records, 11
shutouts, 21
sidelines, 9, 27
Smith, Bruce, 16–17
Smith, Emmitt, 16
soccer, 5
Super Bowl, 7

tackling, 12, 14, 24, 25
time-outs, 13
touchdowns, 4, 5, 11, 15, 16, 21
touch football, 24, 25

Women's Football League (WFL), 19
Women's Professional Football League (WPFL), 19

yard lines, 9

ABOUT THE AUTHORS

Katie Marsico worked as a managing editor in children's publishing before becoming a freelance writer. She lives near Chicago, Illinois, with her husband and two children. She'd like to dedicate this book to her son and future football star, C. J.

Cecilia Minden, PhD, is a former classroom teacher and university professor who now enjoys being an author and consultant for children's books. She lives with her family near Chapel Hill, North Carolina.